MACHINES AT WORK

In the Air

IAN GRAHAM

QED Publishing

First published in the UK in 2006 by
QED Publishing
A Quarto Group company
226 City Road
London EC1V 2TT
www.qed-publishing.co.uk

A catalogue record for this book is available from the British Library.

ISBN 978 1 84538 899 7

Written by Ian Graham
Produced by Calcium
Editor Sarah Medina
Foldout illustration by Ian Naylor
Picture Researcher Maria Joannou

Publisher Steve Evans
Creative Director Zeta Davies
Senior Editor Hannah Ray

Printed and bound in China

Picture credits

Key: T = top, B = bottom, C = centre, L = left, R = right, FC = front cover

Active Flight Systems 4; **Air Canada** 16; **Airbus S.A.S**/2005 11, 21, /2006 17B, 17T, 20B, 31B;
Alamy Images/Allen Fraser Photography 8–9, /Stephan Goerlich 10–11, /Robert Harding World Imagery 6,
/Pierre Manning 27, /Steve Mansfield-Devine 22–23; **Bell Augusta Aerospace Company** 15T; **Bombardier Transport** 9T;
BruceAir 23; **Commonwealth of Australia** 3; **Corbis** 20T, /Richard Cohen 26–27, /George Hall 16–21, /Reuters/Darrin
Zammit Lupi 24, /Martin H. Simon 28–29 /Jim Sugar 30–31; **Department of Defence Visual Information Center**/
United States Airforce 12–13; **DG Flugzeugbau GmbH** 7; **Eurocopter** 14–15; **Getty Images**/AFP/Pierre Verdy 26,
/Imagebank 4-5, /Stone 22, /Workbook Stock 6–7; **Gulfstream Aerospace Corporation** 9B; **Lockheed Martin
Corporation** 15B; **NASA** 29, 32, 33, /Nick Galante/PMRF 32–33; **Northrop Grumman Corporation** 13;
United States Airforce 12, 24–25; **Virgin Atlantic Global Flyer** 31T

Words in **bold** can be found in the Glossary on page 34.

CONTENTS

IN THE AIR

Every day, thousands of aircraft soar into the sky. There are all sorts of aircraft, and they are used for lots of different purposes. Some are just big enough for the pilot, and only make short flights. Others carry hundreds of people half way round the world. **Airliners** carry passengers and **cargo** planes transport goods and materials between the world's biggest airports. Search-and-rescue helicopters help people in trouble, and **experimental** planes test new ideas.

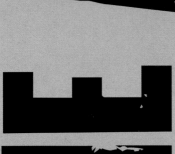

▲ A paramotor pilot steers by pulling control lines to change the shape of the parachute.

KEEP IT SIMPLE

The simplest aircraft with an engine is a paramotor. Its engine is very small, and it drives a propellor that has a metal frame around it. The pilot straps the engine to his or her back and hangs under a wing-shaped parachute, called a paraglider. The pilot uses a hand controller to make the engine go faster or slower.

Building planes

Airliners are very complicated machines. Each one is built from many thousands of parts. First, large pieces of each plane are built separately, and then cranes bring these pieces to one place so that they can be joined together. After this, the electrical and **control systems** are added, and the engines are fitted. Finally, the seats are put in and the plane is painted.

▲ This building in Washington D.C., USA, is where Boeing airliners are put together. It is the world's biggest building.

◄ Today, there are about 25 000 airliners flying passengers around the world.

FACT!

The Boeing assembly building is so big that more than 2000 houses could fit inside it!

FUN PLANES

Flying a plane is great fun. Lots of planes are flown simply because their pilots enjoy flying so much. Many pilots fly very small planes. These planes have engines that work like car engines, but they drive a propellor instead of wheels. Some pilots like to fly planes called **gliders**. They do not have any engines at all, and they glide through the sky like a bird!

Pilots learn to fly in small ➤
aircraft like this.

▲ This is one of the many different types of microlight and ultralight aircraft flying today.

MICRO FLYING

The smallest planes are called microlights, **ultralights or light sport aircraft. It is easier for people to afford one of these planes of their own. The simplest microlights have an open frame, with a seat and an engine. Others have a covering over the body and** cockpit.

Sailing on air

How do gliders fly if they do not have engines? A glider is often towed into the air by a cable attached to another plane. The cable is released when the glider is flying. The pilot then looks for **air currents** to carry the glider higher and to keep it flying for longer. To land, the pilot glides back to the ground.

A glider's long thin wings are ▲ a great shape for soaring.

FACT!
Planes are very expensive to buy, so some pilots spend hundreds of hours building their own plane from a kit!

BIZ-JETS

Business people sometimes choose to travel in small planes called **business jets**, or biz-jets, so they can fly at a time that suits them best. Most biz-jets carry four to ten passengers. They can fly into small airports where bigger airliners cannot land. Even though they are small, biz-jets can still cost millions of pounds. Some businesses cut the cost by sharing biz-jets, or by hiring them just when they need them.

Gulfstream

The Gulfstream 100 is a business jet with room for two pilots and up to seven passengers. Its power comes from twin **jet engines** at its rear. It can fly from New York to most airports in North America. From Rome, in Italy, it can reach airports in Europe, Scandinavia and North Africa.

◄ The Gulfstream 100 is the smallest of the Gulfsteam business jets.

FLYING OFFICES

It is hard for passengers to do any work in a crowded airliner. But business jets can be used as flying offices. Meetings can be held and office work done during a flight. The passenger cabin may be quite small, but there is enough room for comfortable seats and tables to work on.

▲ A biz-jet cabin is very small compared to an airliner, but it is very comfortable and convenient.

N181CJ

CitationJet

▲ The CitationJet is a light business jet for journeys up to 2750km.

FACT!
There are more than 20 000 business jets flying in the world today.

CARGO PLANES

Every year, tens of millions of tonnes of cargo are moved around the world by air. Products and materials can be moved quickly over large distances in planes. Fresh food and flowers can be delivered to almost anywhere in the world within a few hours, so they arrive in perfect condition. Most air **freight** is carried in the cargo **holds** of airliners. The rest is carried by cargo planes. Some cargo planes are airliners that have been converted to carry freight instead of passengers. Others have been specially designed to carry cargo.

Aircraft are loaded ➤ with cargo packed into metal containers.

cargo container

Super transporter

The Airbus A300-600ST Super Transporter has the biggest cargo hold of any aircraft. It is such an enormous plane that it is also called the Beluga, after a large type of whale. The Airbus Super Transporter is a specially modified Airbus airliner. It carries parts of other Airbus aircraft to the factory where the planes are put together.

▲ Airbus has five of these huge transport planes.

FACT!

The world's biggest **mass-produced** cargo plane is the Antonov An-124 Ruslan. It is built in a country near Russia, called the Ukraine.

WARPLANES

Planes play an important role in war. Different types of warplanes do different jobs. Fighters attack other planes, bombers attack targets on the ground and fighter-bombers can do both of these jobs. Special spy-planes are used to find out information that might help to win a war. The latest warplanes are made from materials that do not show up well on **radar**, which is used to spot enemy planes. These planes are called stealth planes. The F-22 fighter and B-2 bomber are stealth planes.

21st-century fighter

The F-22 Raptor is the world's newest fighter plane. It started flying with the US Air Force at the end of 2005. It can fly at twice the **speed of sound** up to 15km above the ground, and is designed to out-fly any other fighter it might meet in the air.

The big opening ➤ on each side of the F-22 takes in lots of air for the plane's engines.

air intake

cockpit

▼ The F-22 fighter is a stealth plane. It is powered by two jet engines.

▲ The Global Hawk spy-plane has not got a cockpit, because it does not need a pilot!

ROBOT PLANE

The Global Hawk is a spy-plane without a pilot! Its computers are programmed with a mission before it takes off. The Global Hawk carries out the mission and then returns to base all by itself. It can circle over one spot for up to 24 hours – far longer than any plane flown by a pilot.

FACT!

In 2001, a Global Hawk spy-plane flew itself 13 840km, from the USA to Australia.

HOVER FLIES

Most aircraft have to move along the ground very fast before their wings can lift them up into the sky. These aircraft need a long, straight runway to help them to get into the air. But there are some aircraft that can fly straight upwards and even **hover** in one place. Some of these aircraft are planes, but most of them are helicopters. A helicopter's **rotor blades** whirl around like long thin wings to lift the aircraft straight up into the air.

FACT!

The Harrier Jump Jet was the first successful military **vertical** take-off plane.

AIRLINERS

Every year, nearly 2 **billion** people fly in an airliner. The biggest airliners fly people on the busiest routes between the world's largest international airports. Smaller planes fly between both international airports and smaller airports in different areas or cities. For about 30 years, the world's biggest airliner has been the Boeing 747. It is so big that it was quickly nicknamed the **Jumbo Jet**, after a famous large elephant. The biggest type of Jumbo Jet is the Boeing 747-400.

Boeing 777

The latest Boeing airliner is the 777. It was the first airliner designed totally on computers, without any drawings made on paper. When the first Boeing 747 was produced in the 1960s, it needed 75 000 paper drawings! The designers of the new 777 could move its parts around on computer screens to check that they fitted together before the plane was built.

▲ The Boeing 777 has two of the biggest and most powerful jet engines ever fitted to an airliner.

Airbus A380

In 2005, an airliner even bigger than the Jumbo Jet made its first flight. The Airbus A380 is a giant plane that carries more than 550 passengers on two decks, one above the other. It is so big that there is enough space left over for an office, a gym and even shops! It can fly up to 15 000km before it has to land for **fuel**. When a new airliner is designed and built, it has to have many tests on the ground and in the air before it is allowed to carry passengers. Five A380 airliners made test flights totalling about 2500 hours.

cockpit
where the pilots sit and control the aircraft

▲ The double–deck Airbus A380 is the biggest airliner ever built.

First flight

The Airbus A380's **maiden flight** on 27 April 2005 was a complete success. It lasted nearly four hours. The plane carried a crew of six and about 20 tonnes of test equipment. Experts on the ground watched live pictures sent from the plane's **flight deck**.

More than 50 000 people ➤ gathered at Toulouse, France, to see the A380's first flight.

wings
measure 79.8m
from tip to tip

fuselage
where the passengers
sit – 7.1m wide

AIRBUS A38

windows

Doors

 A fully loaded
Airbus A380
can weigh up
to 560 tonnes.

FACT!
If you want to
buy your own A380
airliner, it'll cost
about £160 million!

Heli-plane

The Bell BA609 Tiltrotor has enormous propellers. This is because they are not just propellers. When the aircraft is on the ground, the spinning propellers lift it straight upwards, like a helicopter. Then the engines tilt forwards and the Tiltrotor flies like a normal plane. The BA609 doesn't need a runway to take off and land.

tilting engine

▲ The Bell BA609 Tiltrotor begins to tilt its propellers to the front so that it can fly forwards.

◄ A helicopter can land almost anywhere. It can land on a road or a field, or even on an oil rig at sea.

FUTURE FIGHTER

The F-35 fighter is an exciting plane for the future. Three different versions of the F-35 will be built: one for the US Air Force, one for the US Navy and another for the US Marines. The Marines' plane will be able to take off and land vertically, like a helicopter.

▲ The F-35B future fighter that the US Marines will use hovers during one of its test flights.

15

GLASS COCKPITS

In the 1970s, airliner cockpits were crammed with hundreds of instruments and controls but, today, you will mainly see computer screens instead. A cockpit with computer screens is also known as a glass cockpit.

Modern airliners have glass cockpits with up to six computer screens. ➤

computer screen

Each wing of a Boeing 747–400 ▲ airliner is big enough for 45 cars to park on.

FACT!
The Boeing 747's enormous passenger cabin is so big that the first-ever plane flight in 1903 could have been made inside it!

COMPETITION PLANES

In the days when there were very few planes, people flocked to air shows and air races to see pilots competing against each other. The winning pilots were as famous as pop stars are now! Air races are still held today. The planes race around an imaginary track in the sky. The track is marked out by towers, called pylons, on the ground. There are **aerobatic** competitions, too. Aerobatic pilots try to fly the best tumbling, looping **stunts** in the air.

FACT!
The Pitts Special stunt plane made its first flight in 1944.

Stunt flying

The Pitts Special stunt plane has won more aerobatic competitions than any other aircraft. It is a biplane, which means that it has two sets of wings, one above the other. It is a very strong plane that can turn and spin in the sky without breaking apart.

◄ There are more modern aerobatic planes, but the Pitts Special can still put on a great show.

EXTRA FUN

The Extra 300 is a modern high-performance aerobatic plane. The pilot can roll it all the way round, from right way up to upside-down and back again, in less than one second! It can perform very exciting stunts.

▲ Its small size, light weight and a powerful engine make the Extra 300 very **nimble**.

▲ Competition planes make a tight turn in an air race.

DISPLAY TEAMS

Pilots usually keep their planes well away from each other for safety. However, some pilots fly their planes very close together on purpose. These pilots belong to display teams of fighter pilots from different countries that put on breathtaking aerobatic displays at air shows. All fighter pilots learn aerobatics to fight other planes in tumbling, turning chases called dogfights. Display teams use these same flying skills to create amazing air displays for big crowds.

Red Arrows

The British Royal Air Force has a world-famous display team called the Red Arrows. They fly red, white and blue Hawk jet trainers. Nine planes take part in the displays, often trailing coloured smoke behind them. The smoke is made by pumping oil and coloured dye into the planes' hot engine exhaust.

The Red Arrows have ▶ given air displays in more than 50 countries.

◀ The US Air Force Thunderbirds team flies F-16 'Fighting Falcon' fighters.

FACT!
At times, the wing-tips of display planes may be only 45cm apart.

LIGHTER THAN AIR

The first aircraft that people flew in were hot-air balloons and **airships**, which are known as Lighter Than Air (LTA) craft. LTA craft rise up into the sky because they are lighter than air. Airships are filled with a very light gas called helium. Hot-air balloons rise because they are filled with air that is hotter than the air around them. The pilot heats the air inside the balloon with a gas flame.

Airships today

The Zeppelin NT is a modern airship made in Germany. Up to 14 people, including two crew members, sit in a cabin called a **gondola**, underneath the airship. The weight of the airship is balanced by the lighter-than-air helium gas inside it. The airship is made to take off or come down again by tilting its propellers up or down.

▲ The Zeppelin NT airship made its first flight in 1997.

HOT AIR

Hot-air balloons drift silently with the wind. The pilot and passengers stand in a basket under the balloon. The pilot makes the balloon climb by turning on a gas flame to heat the air inside the balloon. Turning the flame off lets the air cool, so the balloon goes lower again.

Most balloons are round, but they ➤ can be made in all sorts of shapes.

gondola

FACT!

In the 1930s, wealthy people travelled between Europe and the USA in enormous luxury airships.

▲ Airships are used to keep an eye on traffic and to film important events on the ground below.

SPECIALS

Most aircraft are made in hundreds and thousands but, sometimes, just one or two aircraft are needed for a special purpose. Some of these planes are made by adapting existing airliners. The US President flies in one of two specially adapted Boeing 747s. When the President is on board, the plane is called Air Force One. It has a crew of 26 and it can carry about 70 passengers. Instead of rows of seats, it has a dining room, offices, bedrooms and a shower.

White Knight

SpaceShipOne

▲ The White Knight plane carries the SpaceShipOne spaceplane underneath it.

KNIGHT FLIGHT

Sometimes a plane has to be specially designed and built for the job it has to do. A plane called The White Knight is one of these special-purpose planes. It carried the SpaceShipOne spaceplane 15km above the ground and then launched it into space.

Vomit Comet

Vomit Comet is the nickname of a plane used by **NASA** to let trainee astronauts feel what it is like to be weightless. As the plane dives towards the ground, the passengers float about inside its padded passenger cabin. The European and Russian space agencies have Vomit Comets, too.

◄ Vomit Comet passengers can fly about as if they weigh nothing. It makes some passengers feel sick!

▲ Air Force One is the US President's official plane.

FACT!

The biggest plane ever built is the Antonov An-225. It is so big that it could carry the Russian space shuttle on its back!

LONG-DISTANCE

Aircraft have been setting records for as long as they have existed. There were always pilots who wanted to go faster, higher and further than anyone else. The longest distance records are set by planes that have to be specially built to keep flying for several days without landing. They have to be as light as possible, but also very strong, because they need to carry an enormous amount of fuel for the long journey.

The GlobalFlyer long-distance ➤ aircraft is powered by one small jet engine above the cockpit.

fuel tanks

virgin atlantic

N277SF

FACT!

At take-off, the GlobalFlyer aircraft carried more than four times its own weight in fuel!

Going solo

In 2005, Steve Fossett became the first person to fly around the world non-stop on his own. He flew a specially designed aircraft called GlobalFlyer. In 2006, Fossett broke another record when he made the longest-ever flight without stopping, again in GlobalFlyer. He flew a distance of 42 468km in just over 76 hours.

In 2005, Steve Fossett completed the first ▲ non-stop round-the-world flight in 67 hours.

jet engine

cockpit

Super-liner

Airliners sometimes set records, too. In 2004, an Airbus A340-500 made the longest flight by any airliner. It flew 16 600km from Singapore to New York. It can make such long flights because it has bigger wings and a smaller, lighter body than other liners. It carries so much fuel that the fuel weighs ten times as much as the passengers!

▲ The long-distance Airbus A340-500 could fly non-stop all the way from London to Perth, in Australia!

EXPERIMENTAL

When scientists and engineers want to test a new type of engine or a new shape for a plane, they sometimes build an experimental plane especially for the tests. A famous series of experimental planes are called **X-planes**. They have been built in the USA since the 1940s to test all sorts of new aircraft. The first one, X-1, was the first plane to fly faster than the speed of sound. Other X-planes have tested new vertical take-off planes, jet-planes, **rocket**-powered planes and spaceplanes.

Super-speeder

Today, airliners fly just below the speed of sound. In the future, some airliners might fly as fast as ten times the speed of sound, or about 11 000kph. NASA is using a flying model called X-43A to test the new type of engine, called a **scramjet**, for these super-fast planes.

A future airliner ➤ flying at ten times the speed of sound might look like this.

LOOK, NO BODY!

Future airliners might not have a tail or a body! Instead, passengers would sit inside its wings. This type of plane is called a Blended Wing Body (BWB). So far, only models of the X-48 Blended Wing Body have been made for tests.

A model of a future ➤ airliner is being tested.

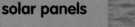
solar panels

▼ NASA's Helios experimental **solar-powered** aircraft makes a test flight.

FACT!

At ten times the speed of sound, you could fly from London, in England, to Sydney, in Australia, in only two hours!

GLOSSARY

aerobatics stunt flying by pilots competing against each other or flying together in an air display

air current moving flow of air

airliner an aircraft used by an airline to fly fare-paying passengers

airship a powered aircraft full of a lighter-than-air gas, such as helium

barge a flat-bottomed boat for carrying cargo

billion one thousand million

blended wing body (BWB) a new type of future airliner that is one big wing with no separate body or tail

business jet a jet-powered aircraft used to provide air taxi and private-flight services

cargo goods carried by an aircraft or other vehicle. Also called freight

cockpit the part of a plane where the pilot sits and flies the plane

control systems parts of a plane that make sections of the wings and tail move in order to steer the plane

experimental for testing. An experimental plane is built specially to test something, for example, a new type of engine or wing

flight deck a compartment in an airliner or another large plane where the crew sits and flies the plane

freight goods being sent from one place to another. Also called cargo

fuel a liquid burned inside an aircraft engine to power the aircraft through the air

glider a plane that flies without engine power by using rising currents of air. Gliders are also called sail-planes

gondola a compartment under an airship for the crew and passengers

hold a space or compartment in a plane for carrying cargo

hover stay in one place in the air

jet engine a type of aircraft engine that burns fuel to produce a jet of hot gas. The force of the jet pushes the plane through the air

Jumbo Jet the nickname for the Boeing 747 airliner, because of its huge size

kit a set of parts to make something

maiden flight a plane's first flight

mass-produced built in large numbers

microlight a small, simple and inexpensive aircraft. Microlights are called ultralights or light-sport aircraft in some countries

NASA the US National Aeronautics and Space Administration, the organization in charge of American spaceflights

nimble able to move and turn quickly and easily

parachute a large sheet of light fabric attached to a harness worn by a person. The fabric opens out as the person falls through the air and slows him or her down to a safe speed for landing

paraglider a wing-shaped parachute

paramotor a motor and propeller worn by a pilot hanging from a paraglider parachute. Paramotor gliders are also called powered parachutes and powered paragliders

propeller a part of an aeroplane that moves the plane through the air by spinning long thin blades in front of the engine

radar a way of finding distant aircraft by sending out radio waves and picking up any reflections that bounce back from the aircraft

rocket a type of engine with its own supply of fuel and also the oxygen needed to burn the fuel. Rockets are extremely powerful and, unlike petrol engines, are also able to work in space where there is no air

rotor blades very long thin wings that spin fast to lift a helicopter into the air

scramjet a new type of jet engine for very fast aircraft that can fly at more than five times the speed of sound

solar-powered power generated by sunlight

spaceplane a rocket-powered aircraft with wings that can soar into space and land again on Earth like an airliner

speed of sound the speed at which sound travels through something

stunt an unusual, difficult and sometimes spectacular act. Stunt flying is also called aerobatics

vertical straight upwards

wing part of a plane with a special shape that lifts the plane upwards when it moves through the air

X-planes a series of experimental aircraft built in the USA to test new ideas for future aircraft

FIND OUT MORE

Websites

Download a book about business planes:
www.avkids.com

Learn how planes fly and how their engines work:
www.aeromuseum.org/eduHowtoFly.html

Build a plane on your computer screen and find out what all the parts do:
www.avkids.com/hangar/smartparts

Learn how to make paper planes:
http://phoenix.gov/AVIATION/kids/airplanes.html